Magic MOMENTS

A COLLECTION OF POETRY

EDITED BY DONNA SAMWORTH

First published in Great Britain in 2016 by:

 Young**Writers**

Remus House
Coltsfoot Drive
Peterborough
PE2 9BF
Telephone: 01733 890066
Website: www.youngwriters.co.uk

Printed and bound in the UK by BookPrintingUK
Website: www.bookprintinguk.com

FOREWORD

Young Writers was established in 1991, dedicated to encouraging reading and creative writing by young people. Our nationwide writing initiatives are designed to inspire ideas and the incentive to write, and in turn develop literacy skills and confidence, whilst participating in a fun, imaginative activity. The final reward is the opportunity for the budding young writer to see their work in print.

Our latest competition, *Magic Moments - A Collection Of Poetry,* focuses on uncovering the different techniques used in poetry and encouraging pupils to explore new ways to write a poem. Using a mix of imagination, expression and poetic styles, this anthology is an impressive snapshot of the inventive, original and skilful writing of young people today. We hope this collection will delight readers for years to come.

CONTENTS

Hillside Primary School, Ipswich

Nettlesworth Primary School, Chester Le Street

Oakdene Primary School, Billingham

Princefield First School, Stafford

St Joseph's Primary School, Newry

THE POEMS

My First Poem

My name is Shianne and I go to preschool,
My best friend is Mason, who is really cool.
I watch Frozen on TV,
Playing with my tea set is lots of fun for me.
I just love spaghetti Bolognese to eat,
And sometimes bubble sweets for a treat.
Pink is a colour I like a lot,
My Frozen toy is the best present I ever got.
My favourite person is Mummy, who is a gem,
So this, my first poem, is just for them!

Shianne Benstock

My First Poem

My name is Finley and I go to preschool,
My best friend is Luke, who is really cool.
I watch Fireman Sam on TV,
Playing with my Frozen doll is lots of fun for me.
I just love beans and sausages to eat,
And sometimes ice lollies for a treat.
Red is a colour I like a lot,
My scooter is the best present I ever got.
My favourite person is Luke, who is a gem,
So this, my first poem, is just for them!

Finley Edward Henderson (4)

My First Poem

My name is Gracie and I go to preschool,
My best friend is Lara, who is really cool.
I watch Winnie the Pooh on TV,
Playing babies is lots of fun for me.
I just love fish from the sea to eat,
And sometimes a sweetie for a treat.
Blue is a colour I like a lot,
My toy doggy is the best present I ever got.
My favourite person is Mummy, who is a gem,
So this, my first poem, is just for them!

Gracie Mary Louise Wren-Marshall (3)

Space

Pitch-black as the deep, dark night.
Silver stars, sharp as a small knife.
Blue glides likes a water slide.
Glistening glow gold and sparkles.
Diamond ring, like a crocodile's back.
Green glow coming out from the distance.
Rockets zooming speedily at rocks.
Hot like the planet Uranus.

Ayesha Hussain (8)

My First Poem

My name is Ella and I go to preschool,
My best friend is Lana, who is really cool.
I watch Peppa Pig on TV,
Playing with babies is lots of fun for me.
I just love ham butties to eat,
And sometimes buns for a treat.
Red is a colour I like a lot,
My Frozen doll is the best present I ever got.
My favourite person is Mummy, who is a gem,
So this, my first poem, is just for them!

Ella Smith

My First Poem

My name is Teddy and I go to preschool,
My best friend is Henry, who is really cool.
I watch Peppa Pig on TV,
Playing on the see-saw is lots of fun for me.
I just love meatballs to eat,
And sometimes an orange for a treat.
Blue is a colour I like a lot,
My horse is the best present I ever got.
My favourite person is Henry, who is a gem,
So this, my first poem, is just for him!

Teddy Tomlins (3)

My First Poem

My name is Luka and I go to preschool,
My best friend is Kyle, who is really cool.
I watch Ninja Turtles on TV,
Playing Ninja Turtles is lots of fun for me.
I just love cottage pie to eat,
And sometimes a Freddo for a treat.
Brown is a colour I like a lot,
My Spider-Man is the best present I ever got.
My favourite person is Spider-Man, who is a gem,
So this, my first poem, is just for them!

Luka Henry Brand (5)

My First Poem

My name is Seb and I go to preschool,
My best friend is Ethan, who is really cool.
I watch Ninja Turtles on TV,
Playing with cars is lots of fun for me.
I just love sausages to eat,
And sometimes grapes for a treat.
Orange is a colour I like a lot,
My monster truck is the best present I ever got.
My favourite person is Mummy, who is a gem,
So this, my first poem, is just for them!

Seb Collett

My First Poem

My name is Jamie and I go to preschool,
My best friend is Daddy, who is really cool.
I watch Pop Art on TV,
Playing with the blue buttons is lots of fun for me.
I just love sausage and chips to eat,
And sometimes a Kinder egg for a treat.
Blue is a colour I like a lot,
My ball is the best present I ever got.
My favourite person is Stainistaw, who is a gem,
So this, my first poem, is just for them!

Jamie Martin John Price (4)

My First Poem

My name is Isla and I go to preschool,
My best friend is Rylee, who is really cool.
I watch a dog game on TV,
Playing princesses is lots of fun for me.
I just love spag Bol to eat,
And sometimes chocolate for a treat.
Red is a colour I like a lot,
My rucksack is the best present I ever got.
My favourite person is Mummy, who is a gem,
So this, my first poem, is just for them!

Isla King

Baking

When I bake a cake with my mum
I have always so much fun

We make cupcakes and the muffins
With all sorts of yummy stuffing

We bake different things together
Despite the freezing weather

Even when outside is sun
I just love to bake with Mum.

Zarah Owczarek (4)

My First Poem

My name is Finlay and I go to preschool,
My best friend is Ewan, who is really cool.
I watch Scooby-Doo on TV,
Playing in my spooky house is lots of fun for me.
I just love chicken and gravy to eat,
And sometimes chocolate bars for a treat.
Blue is a colour I like a lot,
My Iron Man is the best present I ever got.
My favourite person is Ewan, who is a gem,
So this, my first poem, is just for them!

Finlay Lucas

My First Poem

My name is Krithik and I go to preschool,
My best friend is Caleb, who is really cool.
I watch painting on TV,
Playing with toys is lots of fun for me.
I just love dinner to eat,
And sometimes pudding for a treat.
Blue is a colour I like a lot,
My Mr Tumble toy is the best present I ever got.
My favourite person is Mummy, who is a gem,
So this, my first poem, is just for them!

Krithik Mohan (4)

My First Poem

My name is Blakely and I go to preschool,
My best friend is Archer, who is really cool.
I watch Fireman Sam and Thunderbirds on TV,
Playing with cars and Play-Doh is lots of fun for me.
I just love chocolate sandwiches and pasta to eat,
And sometimes marshmallows for a treat.
Red is a colour I like a lot,
My Jupiter fire engine is the best present I ever got.
My favourite person is my Daddy, who is a gem,
So this, my first poem, is just for them!

Blakely Semple

My First Poem

My name is Tegan and I go to preschool,
My best friend is Amelie, who is really cool.
I watch Peppa Pig on TV,
Playing Hello Kitty is lots of fun for me.
I just love pasta to eat,
And sometimes chocolate for a treat.
Pink is a colour I like a lot,
My Peppa Pig plane is the best present I ever got.
My favourite person is my mummy, who is a gem,
So this, my first poem, is just for them!

Tegan Elisa Shearman-Dagge (3)

My First Poem

My name is Tilly and I go to preschool,
My best friend is Grace, who is really cool.
I watch Frozen on TV,
Playing at Grace's is lots of fun for me.
I just love chips to eat,
And sometimes chocolate for a treat.
Blue is a colour I like a lot,
My Elsa is the best present I ever got.
My favourite person is Grace, who is a gem,
So this, my first poem, is just for them!

Tilly Myfanwy John (5)

My Mam

Party-pooper
Food-maker
Sister-watcher
World's worst dancer
Party-planner
Coffee-drinker
Lazy-napper
Messager-mam
Takeaway-eater
House-cleaner
Bedroom-cleaner
Drama-lover
But I still love my mam.

Reece David Debbage Kennedy

Apple

Apple is my favourite treat
Apple is very nice to eat
It's very juicy and makes my heart beat
I grind the apple to get some juice
Sometimes I let it loose
Apple is my delightful treat
I love the colour, it reminds me of the Milky Way
It is so mouth-watering
And is round like a ball
Its seeds are as dark as the night
And it helps me stand tall

Abdussalaam Ishtiaq Khan (8)

Freaky Day

I woke up,
Looked out the window and saw a pup.
I then went to school
And saw a fool.
He was on the floor
Looking at the door.
I looked too at the door,
The door was up high,
Reaching to the sky
Inside the school I walked on the ceiling,
The floor wasn't appealing.
The school was upside down,
But I just said, 'Hi clown.'
It was cool. Upside down school can rule.

Tara Thomas-Krstovic (7)

Space

The alien was the most repulsive beast I'd seen
It had six arms, six eyes and no tongue
It was also so greedy
It had ten legs
Carefully I walked up to it
Cautiously I talked to it.

Mahmood Salih

The Fox

I once saw a fox
It was big, orange and hairy
The first time I looked at it
It seemed very scary.

It was bold
It was dreary
It was fat
Very dangerous in theory!

It was crazy
So mad
And was deadly
So bad

It climbed a big shiny Bentley
I tried to feed it
Very gently
And in the end
It became surprisingly friendly.

Zakariyya Ishtiaq Khan (10)

Untitled

My first day at school I felt like biz phizz.
I saw a teacher and my heart went fizz whizz.
My second day at school was bizz fizz.
My third day at school was good.
My fourth day at school was mad.
My last day at school was fizz whizz!

Chloe Ahmed

The Human Body

T he teeth are as sharp as a piercing knife
H earing your heart beat and drum
E lbow is a strong part of your body

H eads are always thinking day and night
U nder your skin there are incredible bones
M ouths talking every second
A rms help you to do a lot of sports
N ose breathing quickly

B ones are helping us to move quickly
O esophagus helps us eat
D igestion is very important
Y our body must be healthy.

Alex Sierota

Tweet, Tweet, Tweet

I am a little birdie,
I have wings,
I can fly and I can tweet,
Tweet, tweet, tweet . . .

Hadiya Fahad (3)

Indominus Rex

I ndominus Rex is in danger
N othing can stop it now
D inosaurs were real
O h my dear, dinosaurs are here
M an-eating dinosaurs everywhere
I can see
N othing will survive it
U h oh, oh my gosh
S harp teeth to kill its prey

R ather frightened I am
E ats everything in its way
X -rays can not see it.

Jamie Dee Brown (8)

Cats

C urious
A ngry
T rouble maker
S uper.

India Naomi Service (7)

Knights

K illing dragons
N ever giving up
I n the battlefields fighting
G etting ready for battle
H iding behind a bush
T rying to fight
S tretching his arms.

Ella Lumb (7)

Horse

H igh jumping
O ver the fence
R unning
S leeps in a stable
E cho is her name.

Annabelle Pargeter

Superhero

S uper strong arms and legs
U p, up and away!
P owerful laser eyes
E nergy to fight
R unning with speed!
H elping people
E veryone loves her
R eady for action
O ne and only superhero.

Shrivani Amit Naran (7)

Spring

S inging birds flying in the sky
P etals and flowers opening up
R ainbows shining in the sky
I n spring, lambs are born
N ettles and leaves
G irls and boys are playing in the leaves.

Daisy Olivia Wilkinson (7)

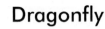
Dragonfly

D angerous fly in the sky
R eally scary in the pie
A t last I have one
G hostly and fun
O n the run
N othing can stop me
F ly away as fast as you can
L ost your way in the sky
Y ou've got to get away.

Calista May Sabatelli (7)

Life In Space

S peedy spaceships zooming through the sky
P eople waving and saying goodbye
A stronaut floating on the moon
C rashing comets, see them zoom
E verything up there has no gravity, but when your rocket lands you will
definitely see me.

Ceiran Bradford (10)

The Island Of Jamaica

J oyous blue sea washing the little boats
A eroplanes are the only way to get there
M agnificent views all around
A ll the people enjoying the sun
I f you get the chance, be sure to take it
C aribbean fruits are juicy
A Caribbean sunset is beautiful.

Harry Mason Vaughan (7)

Alfie

A is for Alfie
L is for little
F is for four
I is for I can see
E is for elephant.

Alfie Michael Emanuel (4)

Mum, Dad, Sisters

M y mum is very helpful to me
U sually she smacks me a lot
M e and my mum go out

D ad is always there for me
A nd always hugs me
D oes everything for me

S isters are really cute
I f your sister is sick you go and hug her
S isters love you and you love them
T en years after they are older
R eason why you have a sister is to love her
S isters love you.

Zhuri Lydner

Jamaica

J uicy mangoes, pineapples, kiwis
A famous person Bob Marley
M any banana trees
A mazing country
I t's miniature
C ave River
A round water.

Darci Hall

Horrid Henry

H orrid boy
O n the loose
R ude boy
R ude and rough
 I t's never a good day for him
D angerous kid

H omework, not in all the time
E nough with the noise
N ot enough work all the time
R uins his room
Y ells at his mum.

Janiyah Kay-Deann Aneliese Malcolm (7)

Summer

S unny and bright days
U nder a tree is nice shade
M any wasps and bees come to play
M any people like to stay
E ating food is good today
R acing is nice to play.

Deanne Quaye

Butterfly

B eautiful wings.
U p in the sky.
T wo eyes to see on their head.
T wo antennae.
E at nectar.
R ainbow colours.
F lowers to drink from.
L ong tongue to help it drink.
Y ou enjoy flying.

Kieran Mark Kirby Harrison (6)

Magic

M onsters are scary
A pple trees blow in the wind
G iants scary and tall
I ncredible princes attack the dragon
C olourful rainbows are magic.

George James Metcalfe

Fairy Tales

F ire-breathing dragons fight evil dragons
A dventures in Once Upon A Time Land
I ncredible fighting knights
R iding horses is fun
Y ucky food for ogres

T rees are still in the night
A pple trees are poisonous
L isten and you will hear growling, big, brown bears
E xciting adventures
S leeping Beauty being saved by a handsome prince.

Cooper Smith

Aliens

A s round as a round circle
L egs are red as a juicy tomato
I am very shiny, I don't like humans
E ats what he can get his red hands on
N ose as sharp as a point
S loppy, slimy, red legs.

Leigha Weston (10)

Baby Polar Bear

B aby polar bear so small,
A time will come and you will be tall,
B y your mum, you like to play,
Y ou meet new friends every day.

P rey of fish
O n your dish.
L arge danger comes, your mum must fight,
A lways gives you a fright,
R eady like a cheetah to run.

B y your mum you like to sleep,
E ach night you sleep with no peep.
A fter a few years you'll be grown up,
R unning after your polar bear pup.

Destiny West

Summer

S is for sunshine, bringing ecstasy and love,
U is for ultra-special, because summer is what I dream of,
M is for magical, butterflies fluttering in the air,
M is for memories, memories of a summer fete,
E is for eating, especially ice cream!
R is for romantic, summer is my happy dream . . .

Harshini Amarnath

Outstanding Moon

O utstanding moon
U nder the shining sun
T he bright sparkling stars

O pen to roam free
F rom the sun to the moon

T his is my world
H appy shining sun
I saw a cold planet called Pluto
S aving Saturn

W hite icebergs on Earth
O range flames coming off the sun
R ed flaming sun
L ooping planets
D eafening flames of the sun

I nspirational science
N emesis aliens
T errifying, no air in space
O pen space for miles on end

T he burning flames from the sun
H igh in the sky are gleaming stars
E normous sun

G reat, powerful gravity
A mazing Pluto so small
L ater on in the day I was in space
A mazing stars in space
X enophobia of aliens
Y esterday I was on Earth but now I'm in space.

Gregor Sands (10)

River Of Tears

Cry of sins,
A life of sorrow,
Hollowness sphere,
Fate passing by,
Stance of silence,
Distance in-between,
Weeping of shame,
Photo in denial,
Pain of pessimistic,
Crime of innocence,
A river of tears,
That can withhold,
Any kind of night.

Isra Sulevani (12)

Aliens

Saucer flyer,
Moon lander,
Space raider,
Planet bouncer,
Human zapper,
Science whizz,
Futuristic beings.

Holly Burns

War Makes You Sore

I can feel myself slowly fading away
There is lots of dirt
I can see the lovely poppies sway
War - it always leaves you hurt.

I can see a swooping plane
I can see a big green tank
War is causing a lot of pain
My heart has already sank.

I am in a very dirty trench
I am all skin and bone
My hands manky in a clench
I know now I am all alone.

Chrissie Ramage MacKinnon

Deadpool

Deadpool loves to play and eat,
But never likes to cheat,
And usually likes to sleep.
He is very funny and hates getting beaten in races.
Some people describe him as crazy
And he is not to be trusted.
Deadpool is sneaky and very cheeky.

Callum Kai Lam Fung (11)

Cars, Motorbikes And Jets

Is a Ducati faster than a Bugatti?
Is a Ferrari faster than an army truck?
Will a Corvette be faster than a jet?
Will a Porsche give you torture?

A Porsche Cayenne is a good car,
When you are in it you look like a superstar.
A Porsche Cayenne's wheel is lighter than steel,
Its interior is superior.

A BMW M6 is the best car,
If you explore it you will think it beats the rest.
It has a nice smooth floor and really nice doors,
It is the best car ever so it will never bore you.

All the cars are very nice,
They are not as slow as mice.
I really like the cars,
If you like them you will be the superstar.

Aryan Verma (9)

The Light

As darkness falls,
the lights beam down,
on everything around.

No one is out,
but they are about,
smiling down upon us.

The wind whispers in our ears on the cold night,
they guide us through the filthy streets,
they are the only light.

Home welcomes us back in,
all warm and cosy.
What a horrible night that was.

The sun rises at dawn,
the village comes alive.
If it wasn't for the light that night,
we wouldn't have survived.

Coral Isla Thomas (12)

Rain

Just me and the rain,
I sit here and I think about all the people locking themselves inside because
of it.
Why does rain have to make people sad?
Do people not like looking out of their windows in their cosy, warm houses
and seeing bright glowing lights on cars and buses?
Big, tall buildings staring into the sky,
I see a dark blue sky with little thin wet drops coming out from it.
The puddles in the streets are glinting and glowing
with the reflection of the moonlit sky.
I see many people running with books and newspapers on their heads and
big umbrellas. The colours on the umbrellas are black, rainbow and purple.
Big, tall buildings staring into the sky,
I can now hear thunder roaring across the world.
It makes the dogs howl, the cats miaow
and the hedgehogs curl up in to little spiky balls.
Once again there are people running into their homes
to try and stay warm and dry.
Big, tall buildings staring into the sky,
I now see smoke coming out of chimneys,
The rain has now stopped, will it ever be back again?

Megan Kingston (9)

Liechtenstein

Liechtenstein is the best
Inspires me with his art
Especially when he uses spots
Colours he uses are always bright and awesome
He is very good at drawing
Teaches me what I can experiment with
Encourages me
Never have I complained about a single picture
Spots and lines are a really attractive way of drawing
Talented
Every piece I produce, I always aim higher
Independently I am learning new styles
Never give up using Liechtenstein's work; I will become a great artist!

Jazmine Mead (10)

The Fireworks

Boom, boom!
The fireworks burst into the dark black sky.

Bang, bang!
The fireworks finish and grey clouds come out like steam coming out of a train.

Pop!
The fireworks begin again and people look out their windows
It's just so fascinating to see!

Myesha Hoque

Online

I am nothing.
A frail soul
No one cares about me
I have no one
No friends
No family
No life
They don't care what I think
What I feel
My existence itself is a waste of space
A waste of money
A waste of love
They think my happiness is fake
They think I cry for attention
If only they knew the truth
They think I'm capable of nothing
That I simply just sit there like a doll
But inside
Inside I am angry
I am a tsunami crashing down and destroying cities, towns
I want to scream
To shout
To yell and punch
But I can't
I remain calm
Composed
I can't break
I can't snap
But not all is bad
Although everyone hates me
I have music
Where everyone has something mean to say
Music has something deep
And even though everyone around me is horrible
I have other people
People who are my friends
People who are kind
Caring

Maybe I'll never see them in real life but online
Online they'll always be there
Always be there to make me laugh
Make me smile
As long as I'm online they'll be real
By my side.

Baidehi Sarkar (13)

Spring

Spring, oh spring I love the word
Spring, spring when sheep come out in herds
I finally feel a spring breeze, while collecting up sweet peas
Spring, spring is when I was born
Just look at all of the bright yellow corn.

The pink and white blossom growing on the trees
Tiny buds turning into beautiful leaves
As I am sitting in my striped garden chair
My mum picks lots of pears
Tiny chicks huddle in their nests
Whilst blankets of bluebells cover the forest
Daffodils lined up all in a row, smiley faces always glow
The bright green grass growing in the sun
Whilst lots of children are having fun
The rippling, blue, shimmering rivers
It is so beautiful it gives me the shivers

We shall be delighted by all these lovely things in spring.

Lillie May Downton (8)

Silence

The sound of silence
Is when time freezes,
Is when there's nothing around you,
That's the sound of silence.

The sound of silence
Is when hope is dying,
Is when the world has ended,
That's the sound of silence.

The sound of silence
Is when all you love is lost,
Is when the poem has ended,
That's the sound of silence.

Aiyana Poppy Gordon

The Fire Dragon

Fire-flicker
Meat-eater
Egg-stealer
Air-glider
Flying-glider
Scary-ride
Fish-eater
Tail-swooper.

Bailey Willis

Senses At The Seaside

I hear waves crashing,
Children splashing,
Seagulls squawking,
Adults talking

I feel the sand against my skin,
Grandad don't drink too much gin,
I feel the sun against my back,
The donkey's fur is as rough as a racing track

I taste the chips, as salty as the sea,
It makes my taste buds tingle with glee,
The ice cream is as white as snow,
The pasties might taste nice, who knows?

I smell fish as fresh as a new car,
My dad's pint of lager,
The blobs of donkey poo along the sand,
Hope I don't get it on my hand

I see seashells dotted around,
I think it's time I was homeward bound,
I see Jamie's bucket in front of me,
Quick, here comes the sea!

Charlotte McCammon (10)

Are We Real

Are we real, if we are what are we?
What is life living? How did we get here?
I am transfixed by the sublime beauty of eternity.
Specks of dust twinkle and microscopic raindrops evaporate,
The colours leisurely revolve.
The shooting stars rapidly whoosh across the sky like a bullet
It's mesmerising, cloudy, glistening,
Inky dark all at the same time,
The colours whirl like dropping paint into a water pot.
The stars shatter into specks of dust,
Looking up to the sky,
I feel spellbound by the glittery moon,
The mesmerising, majestic Milky Way dances delicately like a ballerina,
When will we know? . . .

Sophie Carpenter (10)

Awesome Dad

My dad is awesome
You see him whilst he reads the paper
Strong and calm through the windowpane
Dads are fantastic but mine is the best
He is always there, to listen and answer my all questions.

Danger is far away when Dad is near
Doing what he does in the best way.
You have to admit my dad is really awesome.
Do not forget our dads because they are cool carers too . . .

Lauren O'Reilly

Brave And Brutal

Down in the trenches, we are all weary.
The dark and gunfire making it all scary.
When we go out on the land so bleak.
Some soldiers dead, some soldiers weak.

All of us out there fighting, my friends so heroic.
Some people at home thinking this is all ironic.
Some soldiers dead lying in a heap
Going to have to take the risk and leap.

Some of my friends out fighting, always so daring.
Hearing the gunfire up above is always scaring.
Down in the trenches it is always cold.
Me and my friends are always bold.

Nehan Seneviratne (8)

The Sea

High up on the mountain you can hear the fountain.
You can see the dark blue sea.
Then come back down to the houses for tea.
Calm is all around, now there is not a sound.

James Sykes (6)

Who Am I?

I am a surprise
I don't have eyes
I'm wrapped in plastic
I am fantastic
I could be red
But I'm not dead
I could be blue
Bluer than you
I could be pink
But I don't think
Make up your mind
I'm not hard to find
You could put me in a milk bar
Or eat me in a car
I do not walk
I do not talk
But most of all I don't like pork
I am shy
I do not cry
I will never let out a wimpy sigh
I find myself covered in spit
Then fall into a bottomless pit
Serena Williams likes my taste
But doesn't like tomato paste
Do not be scared of me
All I want is to be free
I am very nice
I like the taste of rice
Do not fear
I do not like beer
You can't cut me into slices
I'm filled with sugar
But don't think I'm a booger
When I'm around every one will cheer

People will stop
When I am in a shop
You'll buy me five times over
Now who am I?
Freedom.

Mariam Uddin (8)

My LOL Poem

Oh . . . The LOL had a doll
That was called Sindol
And wanted a friend
That hoped it wasn't the end
And the LOL had lollipops
That were called Snops

The doll had some too
And he also broke through!
That is the end
And LOL will be your friend.

Luca Feltrin (7)

Danger, Danger Is Everywhere

Danger, danger is everywhere!
On the ground and in the air.
In the sea and high up in the clouds.
Where it's quiet and where it's loud.

Danger:
You might have your bottom bitten by a toilet shark.
You might get catapulted off the swing when playing in the park.
You might summon a herd of stampeding elephants when you play a drum.
On page 9 you might find a deadly scorpion that squirts poison from its bum.
There might be a family of crocodiles living in your pond.
A wizard might cast a bad spell on you with his magic wand.
You might cut off your finger on the sharp corner of a book.
Your cat might be a tiger cub, better take a look.

So:
Look and listen from morning to night.
And hopefully you'll survive and be all right.
Keep yourself safe and please take care.
Because danger, danger is everywhere!

Elliot Owen (8)

Cedric The Snail

Cedric the snail is surprisingly sleek
He munches on oysters, his tantalicious treat
He moves with such sprite, he's amazingly fast
But this fateful Friday would alas be his last

It started as always with slug slime when he woke
And a giant piece of kipper to dip in his yolk
He gargled with root beer
And flossed without fear
He always saved afters
For later in the year

He dressed in his wellies with a fig leaf for a cloak
He really was handsome - and that's not a joke
He set off on his travels, it would take him all day
To travel to work was a garden away

The shadow was upon him, it blocked out the sun
Sadly for Cedric his demise had begun
The raven swooped down and plucked him with ease
Then carried him gracefully up through the trees
The chicks were all waiting hungry in the nest
Cedric dropped in - you can guess the rest.

Callum Cavanaugh

My Beautiful Thoughts

Staring out the window,
Wondering what to do,
Eyes that feast upon the world,
Listening to music as time flew by,
Looking at the sun setting,
Looking at the clouds,
Going on their adventure to the horizon,
It is a rainy day,
After bed when everything is still,
I look at the peeking stars,
And say to myself I wish I had magic.

Mikaila Anna Mathew

Spring

S weet smells through the air
P retty flowers every where
R eally sunny days
I ce lollies to cool down
N ice flowing breezes and
G ardens really tidy.

Sineidin Tamakloe (8)

Nature Senses

Caterpillar, caterpillar what can you see?
I can see a flower with a bumblebee!
Bumblebee, can you tell me what do you feel?
Softness of petals is what I can feel.
Can you also tell me what did you taste?
I tasted nectar, no time to waste!
Flower, now that the bee is gone,
Can you hear a lovely song?
Nothing lovely here to hear,
Just a frog who is croaking near.
Froggy, froggy, when the wind blows,
Can you smell a lovely rose?

I played with my senses all today,
Let's tickle them another day!

Sreelakshmi Pradeep (9)

Advent - Haiku

Advent has started
Opening lots of small doors
To find chocolates.

Abi Moorhouse (8)

41

Miss Little Mary

Miss Little Mary,
What are you doing?
Patting the dog,
In a windy fog.

Miss Little Mary,
What are you doing?
Feeding the hen,
In the big old pen.

Miss Little Mary,
What are you doing?
Milking the cow,
Fetch the milk now!

Miss Little Mary,
What are you doing?
Cutting the fur of the sheep,
To go in my blanket to sleep!

Miss Little Mary,
What are you doing?
Patting, feeding, milking, cutting,
What a busy day!
Of course that's what I'm doing!

Rohma Ammar

Untitled

A really big tiger
Looks like a liger
It's so scary
Even a hairy gorilla is scared of it
Its teeth are so sharp
They are like the tips of swords
Its eyes are huge like the sun.

Its claws are sharp as dinosaurs' teeth
Its mouth opens as wide as a person's head
It moves so stealthily to catch its food
It would eat until it bloated up.

Adam Arif

Cheeky Monkey

Monkeys, monkeys all around
Monkeys, monkeys upside down
Monkeys here, monkeys there
So don't forget your hair
So don't forget your chair
Put your monkey into care
And *don't* be scared!

Aisha Hussain (9)

The River Across The Meadow

Follow the grassy path past an overgrown wood,
Plants sway in the cool breeze as they should,
A meadow is there filled with flowers and butterflies of every kind,
The sun shines in your face and for a second you are blind,
A small river trickles over some pebbles,
You see a nest with small eggs that is speckled,
The sun cascades over the ground,
Nature is the only sound,
Stroking the stream with its golden touch,
The sun nurtures everything in the land and cares so much,
The lemon rays wisp between trees,
Like yellow ghosts floating between leaves,
Clear blue water runs slowly down the meadow,
Everything is quiet, still and mellow,
The only sound you can hear is the faint twittering of birds,
You can feel nature speaking to you with no words,
But with the faint brush of wind,
Your happiness has brimmed,
As butterflies whirl around you like a rainbow,
You feel like you are one with nature and not just looking out a window,
You allow yourself to be taken off to another world,
Lying in the soft grass curled,
As the birds sing their last song,
And the sun has nearly gone,
You think of what a lovely day you had,
And how it couldn't be better by a tad.

Luciné Mander (12)

The Freedom Of The Meadow

The freedom of the meadow was breathtaking and tame,
I wondered if the world would ever be the same . . .
The waves encrusting the glazed cut grass,
The gentle water filling in the great mass.
The beauty of the rain trickling down the trees,
The wind whipping around the chimpanzees.

The freedom of the meadow was breathtaking and tame,
I wondered if the world would ever be the same . . .
Beautiful is what the earth can be,
But still there is more to see . . .
Now I realise that I was wrong,
For the earth has much more to the song.

Anshrah Adeel

My Little Sister

My little sister is like a rainbow
My sister lights up my world
Her eyes are as blue as the shimmering sea
Her face is as red as a soft velvet rose
She is so colourful when she is watching over us
She never stops glowing in the night
She never stops glowing when we look at her
We miss you very much
Love from all of us
Lots of love.

Hannah Berwick (11)

A Girl's Life

School, hard work,
Not even a break.
Working till the day is done,
Not even allowed cake,
Get home and you're the servant,
Get ready, feed yourself.
Honestly is this a girl's life,
Or is it a girl's living nightmare?
Help your parents,
Always study,
Not even allowed to chat to your buddy.
No Facebook,
Or even Snapchat,
Honestly I feel like I could backchat.
Then they say, 'No attitude,'
Really is that my gratitude.
No phone, laptop or even Tablet,
Really is there any social here.
Too young to even drink beer.
Is this what life is about,
Full of rules to obey.
On top of this still no cake.

Zainab Iqbal (12)

That Feeling!

From the moment I was born,
I knew there was going to be that time
where I'd have to become a mature and sophisticated woman!
Who cooks, clean and works but little did I know
that there was a dreaded time hidden in the future
that's named 'Puberty' which prepares you for your adult years!
I fear the sense of growing up and when the moods kick in!
Although I am 11 nearly 12 sometimes I feel so small
trapped in a big world full of decisions
to make my life a better place!
But sometimes I think, it won't hurt to be a little childish sometimes
where I can still dance on my bed in pyjamas
singing into my black 'Tony' hairbrush!
You have to learn that growing up doesn't always make you cry,
it's just life, so be happy and don't forget to smile!

Ffion Sara Jeffery (11)

Enjoy

As hard as a brick, as soft as wool,
As wiggly as a snail, as slow as a slug,
As fast as a racing car, as sweet as chocolate,
As wet as a river, as beautiful as a sunflower, as blue as the sky.

Ridwaan Ibn Abdulnoor (7)

Chocolate Cake

Chocolate cake, chocolate cake
As yummy as can be
It's very fun to bake
Sometimes that's all I can see
Chocolate cake, chocolate cake
Delicious for me
It's so tasty for goodness' sake
When eaten, I feel free.
Chocolate cake, chocolate cake
As brown as can be
All its funny wrinkles
Look amazing to me.
Chocolate cake, chocolate cake
Sometimes square, sometimes round
It even comes with a flake
Out of the oven it comes with a sound.

Tharuki Dhanapala (7)

Charlie's Senses Poem

Popcorn looks like fresh little clouds
It sounds like pop, pop and bum, bum
When it's in the microwave
Popcorn feels like bumpy roads
It tastes like sweet chocolates
Popcorn smells like yummy pasta
I like popcorn because it reminds me of Toy Story.

Charlie O'Rourke

My Pet Froggy

My pet does not need to be taken out for his walks,
He does not repeat every spoken word so he never talks,
He does not purr like a cat eating fresh fish,
Nor is he blowing bubbles, endlessly in a pond, like a fish,
An amphibian he is; but unlike his friends, his legs will never be found on a French dish.
He's green all over, slippery and slimy but certainly not smelly,
He has a long sticky tongue with which he catches his prey,
He lives on a pond hopping from one lily pad to another just for fun all day,
I hope he doesn't hop off to France one day I pray.
My pet froggy isn't a frog prince under a spell waiting to be kissed,
But if any princess dared he will be sorely missed.

James Brincoveanu

Remember

This is for those in the war,
One of the most bad things ever saw.
But why wear a poppy? I hear you say,
Because of those who fought every day!
Please buy a poppy on Remembrance Day,
So that memory never fades away.

George Thomas Brown (9)

I Will Put In My Box . . .

(Based On 'The Magic Box' By Kit Wright)

I will put in my box . . .
The memories of my precious family.

I will put in my box . . .
The first laugh I made
And the first heartbeat in a million years.

I will put in my box . . .
The glittering sun that shines upon me,
The bottom of the ocean to keep me cool.

I will put in my box . . .
The spring I was born in
And the first leaf that ever fell.

But last of all,
My life that is amazing.

Niya Videnova

My Imaginary Cat

I have an imaginary cat,
He is lazy and scared of bats.
However he is always looking handsome and smart,
But you have to watch out because he might burst and give an unpleasant
fart.
He is no ordinary cat,
He obviously hates rats.
But he loves doing art,
He is good at drawing tarts.
He is friendly and kind,
Also rare to find.

Ameera Rahman

Football

Football is always on my mind
Even more than being kind
You need to pass and then shoot
Give it a giant boot
Do not let the keeper save
Because if you score you will be a fan fave
Keep it up and score some more
Get home, open your door
Turn around more interviews
Which person will you choose?
Saturday morning, next game
Time to earn some more fame
Go, too bad
Come home feeling sad
The fame is not there anymore
You need to push your limits to the core
Keep trying and trying, do your best
You will soon be better than the rest
But it is not that easy
People are sometimes very cheesy
The motto is what I'm trying to say
Keep trying and you'll be the best some day.

Alex Finley Robinson (9)

On The Beach

A place where the sun glares,
A prestigious place that flares,
With people all around,
Enjoying the sun and the ground.

Deep and beautiful sea,
And blue as far as you can see,
The water glistening in the sun,
What everyone enjoys, but one...

Sitting on the side,
Not able to hide,
Is a lonely boy,
With nothing but a toy.

Wearing an oversized shirt,
Which is covered in dirt,
He looks at the water that glistens in the sun,
Which everyone enjoys, but one . . .

Shweta Banerjee (12)

Travelling

I am always on the move
With my sunnies looking cool
Heading to the swimming pool
When the sky is shining blue

Travelling is super fun
When I see a big bright sun
And to get my friends to come
Don't forget to bring my mum

I like to travel by air and sea
I can see fish and coral underneath
Flying around like a busy bee
Watching CBeebies on flight TV

Singapore is full of sunshine
Aussie koalas like to climb
England is filled with ice
Hong Kong is always on my mind!

Jayden Jun Sing Oh (7)

Autumn

Autumn time is on its way for fun
Leaves rustling on the ground
Autumn leaves of different types
So come and run
No more excuses for the sun
No more birds tweeting
Time for wild animals
Autumn time overtakes and it's won

Everyone is running for fun
Animals say it's time for hibernation
Time for hot chocolate and marshmallow
All the work is done.

Hania Naveed Dogar (10)

The Tornado

The tornado is an enraged lion,
Ravenous and red.
He bounces on the fields
Whilst scattering the dead
With his frustrating head
That is the colour of lead.
Hour upon hour he rides,
The malicious, ruthless tides
And cries, cries, cries.
The enraged lion flies
In the horrific night skies.

Connor Stephens (11)

Spring

When the face appears,
We can't but resist,
To unveil our colours,
And show off to the world.

The flying majesties,
High in the sky,
Soar their wings over our heads,
While singing sweet serenades,
We enjoy them swooping along.

And us with our frail arms,
So weak but so beautiful,
How could one be depressed,
In such a scene from Heaven.

It seems for once in our lives,
Our problems blow away,
With the cold, crispy lash.

Shayaan Ahmad (12)

Floods

The flood is a fierce dragon
Enormous and green
He roars on the rocks all night
With his sharp claws
And clashing scales.

Minute by minute he sits and bellows
The loud vicious tones
And groans, groans, groans
The giant water dragon bolts
Rubbing his bloodthirsty belly.

Cody Rose Wiltshire (10)

The Shipwreck

T he current was coming and more merciless than ever before,
H eavily panting the passengers sank down to the majestic sea floor.
E ven though the passengers tried to swim to shore,

S till it didn't work and they all fell to the core.
H owever some of the wrecked ship was still remaining,
I t couldn't be worse . . . until it began raining.
P ieces of the demolished ship were scattered around the sea,
W recked and finished with the only person who survived was me.
R oaring for help but no hope was there,
E ver to be lost, I was in torturous despair.
C oncerned and anxious I knew it was the end for me,
K illed and drowned from the devastating sea.

Eesa Farooqui (11)

Tornadoes

The angry tornado is a spinning shark,
Angry and dangerous.
And he twists round and round
With his snapping jaws and scary roars,
Hour upon hour he twirls,
The ferocious, fearful whirls
And growls, growls, growls,
The enormous shark turns,
Devouring the town below.

Candice Mary Pitman (11)

You Are You

You're the heart, I'm the key
You're the leg, I'm the knee
You're the guitar, I'm the strings
You're the angel, I'm the wings
You're the ignite, in my light
You are you, I am I
You're the sight, in the night
You're my world, in world peace
You're one of the many copious pages;
I'm the rusted isolated book
I'm the food, you're the cook
You're the winter, I'm the snowflake
You're the craft, I will make
You're autumn, I'm the leaves
You're the coat, I'm the sleeves
You are you and I am I
You're the pound, I'm the penny
I'm the less, you're the many
You're the bridge, I'm the troll
You're the person, I'm the soul
I'm the whiskers, you're the cat
You're the human, I'm the hat
You're the flower, I'm the stem
You're 45, I am 10
You're the foundation, I'm the spot
You're the hair, I'm the knot
You're Rapunzel, I'm the tower
You're sweet, I'm sour
A poem by a meek, to a confident girl.

Emma Jane Kingsman (10)

The Picture

My eyes, my eyes, glued to the picture
Free birds flying in a blue tone sky
Large cotton candy clouds shelter those standing underneath their care
Tall green trees have gaps of nets

A dream world is this picture
Pure dairy ice cream in shiny yellow carts with wheels
A kind person hands them out
As the children wear smiles of utter amazement

The orange helter-skelter stands tall
Kids wave at parents, just before they slide down
They slide with cute little rose-red cheeks
Their laugh is infectious

In complete curiosity we watch light pink candyfloss being made from sugar
The green grass swiftly blows and tickles our toes

The horses on classic carousels hop and gallop
Whilst the wind blows off our caps and blows our hair into our eyes
I wish I was part of this picture.

Leanna Miller (11)

The Fire

The fire is a boisterous bull,
Erupting and spitting.
He jumps onto wood; punching and hitting.
With his violent nature and enraged mind,
Hour upon hour he will grind,
The hissing, kissing blazes,
And 'gazes, gazes, gazes'
The boisterous bull lazes
Dies and then goes blind.

Jasmine Read (11)

Fire

The treacherous tornado is an angry bull,
Dark and furious,
He charges on the wrecked environment all night long.
With his pointed jaws and his ferocious brutal horns.
Hour upon hour he claws.

The dreadful, disgusting houses,
And trees, trees, trees!
The disgraceful, enormous bull groans,
Tasting his gigantic horns.
And when the stormy clouds glare
And the rain sniffs in the treacherous rain,
He shudders at his furious feet
And snorts and inhales,
Wabbling his soaked sides on top of the stormy clouds,
And roars and screams fast and furious.

Caitlin Cox (10)

The Blizzard

The blizzard is a vicious bird
Heavy and white.
He flies in the sky all night
With flapping wings and his sharp beak.
Hour upon hour he stalks
The giant snow bird squawks
Clashing his deadly beak.

And when the snow bird moans,
And the white meteors fly in the snowy cloud
He stalks his prey and screeches and flaps,
Catching his motionless prey laying in the deep snow
And cries and screeches far and wide.

Shane Legg (11)

59

Has Spring Come?

Crystallised snowflakes,
Swing to and fro,
Joy brightens winter,
Like sunshine on snow.

Christmas is coming,
Happiness spread,
As love comes to the world,
And wipes out all dread.

Snow crunches under feet,
And blankets the grass,
The wind shakes the windows,
Has winter passed?

Jack Frost sweeps in,
Ice to unleash,
Sunlight appears,
As if to welcome peace!

On Christmas Eve,
We have sleepless nights,
To hear jingle bells,
And see Christmas lights.

Tear off the paper,
Open the box,
What will you get?
A game or new socks?

Boxing Day, Boxing Day,
The day after Xmas,
I wish it was still here,
Oh why has it left us?

New Year's Eve,
A time of gladness,
Last year is history,
And all the winter sadness!

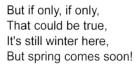

But if only, if only,
That could be true,
It's still winter here,
But spring comes soon!

February, February,
Still winter's alive,
But spring comes next month,
And spring comes alive!

March, March,
Spring's finally here,
Summer comes next,
No winter for a year!

Gabriella Lucia Douglas-Kitsis (10)

My P Poem

My name is Poppy.
I like pizza, pasta,
Pineapple, pancakes,
Plums, pears and
Peaches in my porridge.
Peas, potatoes I prefer,
As parsnips are particularly peculiar!
But, after I pop, puddings,
Pastries, popcorn too.
I hope my poem pleases you.

Poppy Russell (6)

Christmas Cheer

Trickling, tumbling soft snow,
But inside the fires aglow.
Decorating the Christmas tree,
Everyone is as busy as a bee!

Wrapping presents, writing cards
Everyone's finding the work quite hard.
After a while it's time for bed,
Finally I can rest my sleepy head!

Thump! a noise from down the stairs,
Oh, I wonder if it's my sister playing with her toy bears.
Silently sneaking into the hall,
Trying not to slip over my puppy's ball.

What's this I see, a cloud of soot?
An outfit of red and a black polished boot.
A gasp escapes from my wide open mouth,
Is Santa Claus really in my house?

He puts his fingers to his red lips
While eating the snack I left him, potato chips.
Next he is filling our stockings one by one
Clearly having lots of fun!

He takes me outside, into his sleigh,
Soon we're off and I'm screaming yay!
Flying over the moonlit city
I stare in awe as it looks very pretty.

Soon we're off over a white powdery land.
I begin to get frightened, so Santa Claus holds my hand.
In the distance what do I see?
A short jolly man staring at me!

When I get closer I see he's an elf,
Excitement is brewing inside myself.
He unleashes the reindeer and they jump around,
Surprisingly, as they are large animals they do not make a sound.

The man of this season leads me inside.
Where the elves that work there hide.

The smells of the factory are like nothing else,
Machinery oil and newly cut Zelfs.
Candy canes churning inside a large pot,
A kiln in the corner, so very hot!

Sadly it is time to go,
Back to the plain old world we know.
Back in the shiny, sleek sleigh,
Now we're off and travelling far away.

Through the diamonds in the night,
Rudolph's red nose shining bright!
Landing on my snow-covered roof,
Reindeer shaking sleet off their hoof.

Santa Claus says his goodbyes,
Then he's off into the deep, dark skies.
I open the door then creep to my bed,
Being careful where I tread.

Next thing you know, I'm asleep like a log,
Feeling as if I have been on a 100 mile jog!
I will never forget Santa's sapphire eyes watching over me,
And all the magical scenes I have been so privileged to see!

Honor Graham (11)

Getting A Fever

Getting a fever is not something I like
I can't go outside to play with my friends
or ride on my bike
It feels like I'm trapped inside a deadly cage
Burning with fire which resembles my rage
Getting a fever is something I really hate
It feels like the fever monster has used me as his bait
But there is one thing I find very cool
Getting a fever keeps you out of school

Aditya Raje

New Year's Day

The clock is slowly ticking away
Tick-tock, tick-tock
New Year's no further than a day
Tick-tock, tick-tock
Everyone gathered up real close
Tick-tock, tick-tock
Cos being together on New Year's is what matters the most
Tick-tock, tick-tock

Fireworks being held at the ready
Bang! Bang! Bang! Bang!
The clock is ticking slow and steady
Bang! Bang! Bang! Bang!
The minute hand is almost there
Bang! Bang! Bang! Bang!
Let's jump and shout - New Year's almost here
Bang! Bang! Bang!

The night is silent, hushed and eerie
Sh, sh, sh, sh
Midnight close and always nearing
Sh, sh, sh, sh
Just a few seconds until the night is done
Sh, sh, sh, sh
And we are acquainted with the morning sun!
Sh, sh, sh

The clock is slowly ticking away
Tick-tock, tick-tock
The fireworks ready for New Year's Day
Bang! Bang! Bang! Bang!
The silent night is almost done
Sh, sh, sh, sh
As we count backwards down to one.
5
4
3
2
1

Last of all, if I may
There is one last thing I want to say
And that I have written boldly here
My friends . . .

Happy New Year!

Eriifeoluwa Melody Sorinola

Fly

I wonder what it's like to fly,
So high you seem to touch the sky.
The peace, the purity up there,
Above and below, surrounded by air.
See the tiny human bugs,
The cars crawling like slugs.
How small we are on this good, green Earth,
Where we laugh, die, fill with mirth.
I wonder what it's like to fly,
To soar high up in the sky.
But now I must come down to land.
I land upon the soft, white sand.
I'm glad to be back here,
Although it was fun to peer.
Out at our life, our zone,
There is no place, just like home.

Elsa Buerk (8)

Congratulations
your poem has
been chosen as
the best in this
book!

Wind

The wind is a wolf howling, howling for his food.
He creates a tornado when angry,
Stirring up devastation for those in his path.
Tearing through houses with his grey-clawed paws,
Leaving utter destruction.

The wind is a wolf howling, howling for his food.
He ravenously goes out hunting,
For his unsuspecting prey.

If he doesn't get his food, he becomes mad, furious.
We pay the price -
Victims of a natural disaster.

The wind is a wolf howling, howling for his food.

We all like him when he's calm.
A gentle summer breeze keeping us cool.
He loves the attention of the little kids,
Playing in his smooth breath.
The only time our wolf is happy.

Keira Ekpo-Daniels

Solar Eclipse

The solar eclipse was due to start
I felt it in my heart,
But boring as the teachers are
They wouldn't let us see that star!

We went outside full of hope,
I knew that I just couldn't cope,
I looked right up there at the sky
But nothing there could please my eye -
There was just sky!

Everything the teachers taught
Turned out pointless, I thought.
Pinhole camera wouldn't work,
We all felt such a jerk!

It was so windy our papers blew away,
We didn't see them until next May.
We went inside, I closed my eyes
And imagined the eclipse still in the sky,
Maybe next time, I thought with a sigh . . .

Charlie Corbett

FA Cup Final (Aston Villa Vs Arsenal)

Benteke wins a corner, he is in the box
And the ball comes in and he jumps as high as the clouds
He heads the ball in, 1-0 Villa
Chamberlain challenges for the ball successfully
And skips past Vlaar as the last man standing
He is away, chips it, goal! 1-1!
It is injury time with four minutes left
And the Villa goalkeeper, Guzan comes up for the last free kick
Delph launches it in and Guzan's got it in!
In the FA Cup Final, Villa win!

Sammy Ingham

A Winter's Day

Robins freezing as an ice cube perched on a holly branch all alone.
A snowman guarding the house, staring at the window,
Looking through the glass icicles,
Pointy as the end of a picture of the points.
Snowflakes twinkling down like a bunch of sprinkles.
Children in the garden making snow angels.
Houses covered with snow and snow falling off the trees.
Snow cold as water.
Snowy pavements, slippery like some soap.
Leaves falling off trees like smooth feathers.

Lilly Butteriss (7)

The Highwayman

Is she going through the window or through the open door?
I am riding across the highway, over the purple moor.
Do I see her running towards me or is it a cloud full of wondrous seas?
No, it's Bess! My beautiful Bess running, running, running towards me!
Jump on my horse,
And never turn to that horrible house
We are running away to a wondrous land.
But I've got a wondrous plan:
We are going to have a house full of wondrous rooms.
My ear is still full of love.
Making decisions for us!
How are we going to live within kill?
They are after our tail,
Like thunderous hail.
Go, go, go, don't stop . . . never, *no!*

Natalie Mia Ku (9)

Wind

The wind is a ghost of the past.
It washes good memories away.
It takes you to your worst nightmares.
You cannot run, you cannot hide.

The wind is a million people.
The wind will never die.
It has a thousand souls.

Katie Parfett (12)

Under The Oak Tree

I ran my fingers through the long swaying grass
As I leaned back on the humongous oak tree.
I watched the clear sky as a flock of birds did pass
And heard the constant buzzing of a tiny yellow bee.

Calmly enjoying the fresh breeze,
I stared at the world around me.
It felt as though any minute the world would freeze,
But no, I was still sat under the tree.

I breathed in the scent of leaves
As they fell down like parachutes on me.
None of my problems heave,
When I'm under the oak tree.

Mahbuba Faiza Islam (10)

Life

Life is something everyone has to go through,
You may think it's tough but I do too,
I can guide you halfway through
But then you'll have to know what to do,
Because I won't be there forever, neither will you,
So here's a tip you should use,
Open your eyes, see what path calls for you,
Follow it to the end and hopefully I'll see you soon!

Natalia Alicia Bognar

Scarlet Nightmare

The crackle of fire haunts the abandoned city,
A stillness washes over the tranquillity,
The plume from the inferno immerses in the air,
And the hell that is blazing is scattered here and there.

The spawn of wrath commences the fight,
As the screams run throughout the dead of the night,
Scarlet paints the floor and walls,
The shadowy figure roams the halls.

The people watching begin to quake,
Of the deadliest dreams, little demon awake,
The blood moon's rising, begin the war,
The scarlet nightmare begins to restore.

Teagan Marie Hovey (10)

500 Hoses

500 hoses with watery blasts,
With the squirting and spraying it stopped at last.

But that wasn't it, that was not the end
The other 400 sprays their water with no bend.

Soon it came, 200 were down,
Another 200 came without a frown.

Finally all the 200 were out of water,
They went back to the river who loved them like their daughter.

Irfan-Ahmad Olanrewaju Ameen (8)

The Moon's Eye

The moon rises
Surprises the weary day,
Like a Jack-in-the-box
Hello moon.

The moon shines,
Climbs slowly into the stars,
Like a snowdrop following the sun.
Moonlight.

The moon sneaks,
Peeks through the misty cloud,
Like a vicious spy.
That's light.

The moon glows,
Flows in the sky,
Like a frog on a lily pad.
Night light.

The moon creeps,
Peeps into the window frame,
Like a hunting tiger looking for prey.
Night sky.

Kayleigh Terri Robinson (10)

Winter

The wind gently kissed my cheek as it spoke softly
To the snow,
To the trees,
To the grass that was tucked up in bed with a white, fluffy, beautiful blanket.

The tree swayed as he shivered,
Missing the leaves that had been keeping him warm
He was usually a tall dark figure that stood in the park grounds,
Listening to the children around him
But now he was covered in white, wonderful snow
As it tickled him and smiled from his branches and from the ground

The snow glistened beautifully as it gently danced to the ground,
As the rabbits, hedgehogs and badgers were in a deep sleep,
Hidden under the fresh, white, pretty blanket of snow.
They were warm,
I was cold,
But they will wake when spring appears when the newly cut grass is fresh
and green.

Athena Mollie Bruce

Seasons

Winter
As the grey clouds come in,
The droplets of rain bounce down to the ground,
The rain freezes and becomes hail.
The hail hits everyone, 'Ow, owlets get inside.'
Once everyone is inside the hail stops.
Snow starts to fall.
The bare, cold trees have no leaves to keep it warm, brrr!

Spring
The sun starts to shine,
And the seedlings start to sprout,
People's gardens look colourful,
With daisies, tulips, marigolds and petunias,
Lots of pretty beautiful flowers.
The bright flowers can be smelt 100 miles away.
The bees come and the butterflies arrive.

Summer
I can hear cool refreshing drinks being sipped,
Planes zooming off to scorching hot countries.
Summer has finally arrived hooray!
People are having summer parties,
I can smell barbecues, sausages and burgers,
I can see the little children paddling in their pools.

Autumn
The leaves fall off the trees,
Children crunch on the golden yellow leaves beneath their feet.
Children laugh and play all day while they still can,
As the dark nights zoom in at 7pm.
The crusty leaves stay still all night
While everyone sleeps, *zzzz!*

Libby May Thompson (8)

Sun And Moon

When the sun settles down
The moon claims his crown
As he fades into the horizon
Hoping he will get his deserved rest
Only to be woken by the rooster's call coming from within its open beak
Forcing him to come out over the peak
Sometimes he wonders if he will actually get a break
Sometimes he thinks that accepting this job was a mistake
Why didn't this job come with a disclaimer
He was never a worker, more a dreamer
It may sound easy just floating in the sky
But it is very tiring to fly so high
These days I also don't get any respect
In the olden days I actually used to enjoy rising up every day
The sacrifices were good and they were kept daily
Some even sacrificed their family
It's a rare thing to get only one sacrifice monthly
My once loved job is becoming so unbearable
My temper is also becoming unstable
I am starting to hurt the Earth's sources
One day I may leave.

Enian Dhamo (11)

Books

Every book is a treasure,
All of them are beyond measure.
Some bring you pleasure,
While others take you on an adventure.

Like old friends, some share their thoughts,
Whilst others teach you how to play sports.
But my favourite has to be
The one that shows me how to find quartz!

Although you're quiet as can be,
Your mind is buzzing like a bee.
Lost in the world of fantasy,
Where everything can really be.

Max Kupfer (10)

War

War,
Violent and depressive,
Taking your life and turning it into an empty void in seconds.
War is strong - it takes sides with negative things,
And eliminates any good from its fields of pain.
But somewhere hidden among the dead bodies is a light.
It maybe small but it is peace and it can bring down kingdoms
And some day it will overpower war and restore joy to our planet.

Fionn MacMahon (11)

Riddle

I like to perform every day.
I really don't need to pay.
I like to receive gifts.
I can also go up lifts.

I like to encourage everybody.
I even have my own hobby.
I have two big colourful eyes.
I also like to eat pies.

I am an extremely good being.
I use my eyes for seeing.
I share my riddles with the audience.
I can also make a coincidence.

What am I?
A: Original.

Hafsah Nasim (11)

Mum

You are my shadow, for you are the one who is always there for me
You are my reflection, for you are the one I want to be like.

You are the sky, for you are the one I look up to
You are my angel, for you are the one who cares and protects me.

You are my heart, for you are the one who loves me.

You are my mum.

Sophie Child

Rainbows, Sunshine And Flowers

The sun rose up
Like a gorgeous day
No bullies allowed
Ah, so beautiful.

The rainbow shot up from nowhere
It was strange
Let's enjoy the day
With each other.

The beautiful flowers
Are so strange
So fluffy and so gorgeous
They are magical.

Kaitlyn Ann O'Hara (9)

Tanka Poem

Trees like strong metal
Branches are claws gripping you
They stand straight and tall
Slowly the leaves start to fall
Winter is coming quickly.

Abdullah Mahmood

I've Got It In Me

Climb the highest mountain
Swim the deepest seas
Jump off the cliff and fly
Soar through the sky
You've got the power

Make an invention
Make us proud
Invent some wings
And fly with the clouds
I've got it in me
I can do anything I want

I've got magic
But it's not tragic
Because with that
I can do anything I want
It's all I've got in me

Living on Earth
Understanding all the birds
Communicating with words
It's all fantastic

Flying around in space
Going in and out in different ways
I'm lucky because . . .

I've got it in me
I've got it in me
I've got the power right inside
Oh I've always got it in me.

Sathvika Pentrala (9)

Into The Woods

Into the woods if you look closer you will see,
A world of beauty, nature and magic.
Where trees rustle,
Leaves fly,
Flowers prance
And bees buzz.
As stunning as a model and even prettier,
It works to the bone day and night.
As calm as the dead,
As brave as a knight
The woods remain!
Slowly, silently, surprisingly
The wood stays,
And nothing can stop it!

Isabella Mandich

Flowers

Flowers
Colourful, yellow
Blossoming, attracting, brightening
A little surprise outside the window
Crocus.

Ali H Graham (10)

Rain Dance

You said to me
That tears were good
For washing away
Your fears

But why cry tears
When you can be cleansed
Simply by
Dancing in the rain

I guess the point
Of crying is
To release an internal
Pain

But why depend
On flowing tears
When the One above
Can carry your burdens away

So do not worry
For what's the point?
Receive your blessing
And remember to rejoice in the rain.

Opefoluwa Sarah Adegbite (13)

Bullied

Tears are running down my face as I watch them walk away,
I guess I shouldn't worry, it's just another day,
But then I see them laughing, it makes me want to say
'Stop hurting me, they're my friends too, I only want to play!'

But I know I'll get in trouble,
For mentioning her name,
As soon as she knows I've told on her,
She'll call the fire brigade!

I can feel my heart is pounding,
As I watch them in dismay,
Nobody stops by me,
To see if I'm OK.

She makes it feel like a race,
The kind that never ends,
The finish line is miles away,
But all of us need friends.

Minnie Luisa Jacobs (11)

One Snowy Night

I was walking in the snow one frosty night,
There was no one about to give me a fright.
I gazed up at the stars that were shining above,
It reminded me of happiness, joy and love.

Snowflakes were falling onto the ground,
They made a lovely crunchy sound.
Icy puddles filled the street,
It made it slippery for my feet.

Icicles were hanging from the rooftops,
There was even snow soaking through my socks.
A chilly breeze was blowing in the air,
It was blowing all around me everywhere.

Thank you for listening to my poem.
I hope you enjoyed it now that you know it.

Samuel Maybury (11)

Autumn Springs

The flowers are all gone,
The leaves have turned golden brown,
Getting dark early,
Can't really go to the park.

The light is changing,
Leaves are falling off the trees,
They are flying in the breeze,
Picking out leaves from the drain.

Maybe it is starting to rain,
Or is it starting to freeze?
It is feeling colder,
We can smash conkers.

The clocks go back,
Sometimes it is foggy,
Fireworks and bonfires to burn up all the leaves,
Winter is coming up.

Denzil Jory Keast (7)

The Darkness Beneath

You must beware of the darkness beneath,
It lurks in the shadows of every fading light.
Death follows, its best friend,
I'd never forgive even if it just took one.
It's too much of a precious life for it all to end.
But you can't control it, it comes, never to go,
But darkness is not an element, it's not a myth,
It's in everyone.
When loved ones die,
Has darkness caught up with them?
Or has darkness overtaken a being
Who could not resist deadly play?
Stop and think how much life could be saved
If we forbid the darkness
And let it slip away.

Edward Owen (11)

Don't Eat Me!

Look at me! I'm a strip of gum!
I'm the latest invention.
Three courses for your tum.
Fruit bowl, chocolate fudge brownie and milk.
All as delicious as the softest silk.

I'm packed away in a brown box,
Inside a glass jar.
But I'm not on my own.
I'm with my mates.
Who are all packed up,
In lots of little crates.

I'm put on the shelf,
On display.
I've been put next to the lollies
I can see people rushing around with their trollies,
Trying to find me.
I'm the one they must see.

I've been picked out of the pot,
By a boy in a red top.
I can see him with the money.
He will buy me or the honey.

Max Thomas Henry Trewartha (10)

The Opposite Of Peace

As the war rages on I stand still,
The icy wind rushes down my thin, uncomfortable uniform.
My face is covered with mud, dirt and cuts,
My heavy leather boots are broken and torn
So my feet are nearly as cold as my bare hands
And all of this is because of war.
What happens if we die, what happens if we are shot?
Nothing is worth dying for so why is there a war here?
War is against life and happiness,
War gives us death, mourning and injuries
Just to be able to say we won but why compete in the first place?
Guns are fired just to win and bombs are exploding just to be famous
This doesn't seem fair on soldiers
Who are right now sacrificing their lives for us including me.
I have just been shot in the leg by an enemy general.
My heart rate slows down as I collapse onto the ground
My world goes black and my heart stands still, I am dead.
My death, like so many others, is pointless.
An innocent person with feelings like you and me
Doesn't deserve to die for a reason like war.
Even a person who is sinful and vicious doesn't really deserve to die
So why have war? It ruins so many things.

Macy Annabel Merrens (9)

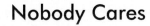

Nobody Cares

Nobody cares,
They never have,
Especially Lewis,
Always complaining I'm depressed,
Yet does nothing just like the rest.
So sad,
So scared
And so alone,
With nobody to listen.
I never speak out at home,
Never wanting to feel more alone.
Tomorrow will be the same,
Nobody will care,
They never will.

Mollie Ella Gregson

Waves

Waves crashing, children clashing,
Grass swaying, love lost,
Silver shining, Mum's eyes glowing,
Lions loud, mice quiet,
Class chatting, vase smashing,
Sheep asleep, an earthquake awake,
Childhood memories, teenage tragedy,
Sun shining in my face,
Never the end of the human race.

Wil Dyer (10)

The Slave Of Suffering

The slave of suffering
Alone. Frightened. Despair. Powerless . . .
The feelings I feel for I am the slave of suffering
I suffer at the hands of those who choose spite and betrayal
I, the slave of every word that means sad
I sit bored with no one. I sit frustrated without hope
I stand chained to a wall, drowning in my own sorrow they brought on
Yet only I am responsible for the tears
Every time I think of laughter and happiness
The knife digs a little deeper to inflict more pain
I've had enough of pain but I can't stop it.
It's there. It's not going away. It's never leaving me . . .
Alone. Frightened. Despair. Powerless . . .
The feelings I feel for I am the slave of suffering!

Eloise Griffiths (11)

Mothers

Mothers give you love.
Mothers are like peaceful doves.
They give you no harm but they are very calm.
They are always by your side so keep that in mind.
They do everything for you so don't argue.
Every mother is unique in their own way.
So we make sure they smile every day.

Rezwan Ahmed (10)

Earth's Elegy

Dear Human Species, you've done it all wrong,
Our friendship never did last that long,
I gave you warmth, I made you strong,
But you betrayed my trust - now we can't get along.
If you heed me now, you can belong
In the unique unity of this universal song.

Okay, you can all stop gawking at this,
You're surely one species I will not miss!
Learn a life lesson from my trees,
They give you oxygen as you please.
But do you give anything in return?
Oh, you people, go live on Saturn!

And what about the other creatures?
To you they are teachers, even preachers!
They are an amazing example to this world,
So important to me, as if they're pearled,
Doing such countless things - can't fit in this poem,
Like gems to me they are, unlike others - ahem.

Yet still, Mankind, you weirdly wonder
Who sends down all that thunder,
Did you ever care to share
My polar bears - no, that's a prayer!
Once they were here, everywhere,
Now are they seen; they're disappearing like air!

You may just have a gifted flair
Although you don't use it - it's very rare!
All your pollution causes a pong
For me, it'll probably last life-long!
Do you ever think about that?
You're all daft - you think I'm flat!

Now I really must sign off,
So don't blame me if you cough
From all the nasty gases you produce
You deserve it, I received such abuse!
So I say 'Yours sincerely, Earth'
Hope you realise what I'm worth.

Nusrat Razzaque (12)

Family And Friends

F orever by your side
A group of people you're always beside.
M y family is oh so great:
 I know there will never be hate.
L ove your family and your friends,
Y ou know they will always comprehend.

A lways appreciate the people who care
N ever know, they may not always be there.
D aily these people may take care of you,

F or they are the people you can speak to.
R ealise they love you more every day,
 I t can be quite hard but what I'm trying to say:
E veryone in your family will always love you so,
N ow this is the thing that they would like you to know.
D elight yourself in them and hug them thankfully,
S o you can show people how much you love your family.

Tahlay-Gabriella Tunani Afobe (11)

Circus

C lowns are silly
I like acrobats
R ingmaster is fun
C lowns are really funny
U nder the tent
S illy juggler.

Jon-Paul Allen (6)
Hillside Primary School, Ipswich

Circus

C heerful clown
I n bright lights that are white
R ed ringmaster
C aptain's colourful hat
U nbelievable clown
S illy clown eating sweets.

Poppy Collins (5)
Hillside Primary School, Ipswich

Circus Tent

C lowns
I n the tent
R ed and yellow
C olourful
U p in the sky
S cary.

John Sewell (7)
Hillside Primary School, Ipswich

Circus

C urly clowns
I nteresting circus
R ound ring
C olourful flags
U tterly amazing acrobats
S hiny sunny circus.

Jamie-Leah Connick (6)
Hillside Primary School, Ipswich

Circus

C olourful tent
I nteresting acrobats
R ingmaster
C lowns are fun
U nder the tent
S hiny lights.

Benny Ciriblan (6)
Hillside Primary School, Ipswich

Circus

C razy clowns
I ncredible funny clowns
R ingmaster in orange
C olourful clowns
U nder a big tent
S uper clowns.

Jaylen Rose (6)
Hillside Primary School, Ipswich

Circus

C lowns are funny
I t is magical
R abbits jumping
C razy clowns
U nder the colourful tent
S uper juggling.

Mia Damljanovic (6)
Hillside Primary School, Ipswich

Circus

Up in the lights . . .

C lowns are colourful and nice
I t's amazing
R ing is excellent
C rusty the clown is brill
U p in the lights
S illy clowns are eating sandwiches.

Logan Cheeseman (5)
Hillside Primary School, Ipswich

The Day We Left

The day we left,
Was full of stress;
The house was left
In a bit of a mess.

The day we left,
We were all in a flap;
My dad got lost
And he needed a map.

The day we left,
We took all the stuff,
The builders' drills were noisy
But we had no earmuffs.

The day we left,
There was a moving van.
And in it,
A big, murky man.

The day we left,
We all got in the car,
It kinda felt like . . .
Yeah, like we were going to Mars.

Then, the day we arrived,
We saw a mouse
But all was well
In our new house.

Jamie Ivory (11)
Nettlesworth Primary School, Chester Le Street

Before It Was Too Late

A man whose son is sick.
Feels like there is a wall so thick.
He has never had the confidence to look for medicine.
The man would never leave his son's side.
His son was glum.
Even though he had never seen his mum.

Then the day came, they knew where to go.
To a gelid place far away where it snowed.
The man told his son and his eyes glowed.
So the man set off with his hiking boots and stick.
He said to his son, 'I'll be back,' and shut the door with a flick.
He adventured far and wide so his son would have pride.
The man ran and found a horse and said, 'I shall ride.'
He rode and rode and rode then he remembered his son would be fine.
He found the gelid place, there was a glow, he had found the medicine.
He picked up the medicine, got on the horse and rode.
He was excited to see his son and got into the mode.
The mode that would get him back faster.
He rode and saw the house on the horizon,
He got to the door, flew up the stairs, his son was not there.

The man had been too late!
The man had been too late!

Caleb Hinnigan (10)
Nettlesworth Primary School, Chester Le Street

Trip To Spain

I woke up in a glum,
But I remembered I was going in the sun.
I jumped out of bed,
'Get up now!' my mum said.

I flew downstairs,
Like a flock of birds,
But I ran into the door.
We all shouted, 'We're going to be late!'

We ran to the car
And drove off, zooming as fast as lightning.
We sprinted in the airport to get our bags on the plane,
At that moment we lost one of the passports,
That second we found it on the floor.

We boarded the plane,
With no time to moan,
But I hurt my bone
And lost my phone.

Dylan John Milburn (10)
Nettlesworth Primary School, Chester Le Street

Splish! Splash! Splosh!

Splash! Splash! Splash! Amongst the waves of a water park.
Bubble! Bubble! Bubble! Under the magnificent glass-clear water.
Whoosh! Down the fastest water slide.
Wow! Relaxing across a rubber ring.

Argh! Lying and tanning on a sunbed.
Cool! A refreshing smoothie in the palm of my hand.
Epic! A beach down the corner to build a tower of strength.

Magnificent, a lovely smell of ice cream and slush.
The best making friends on a hot scorching water park day.
Special you and your family, having the best two weeks on holiday!

Ana Marie Lee (9)
Nettlesworth Primary School, Chester Le Street

Squirrel

S aves food
Q uick climber
U ses claws to eat
I n a tree
R uns fast
R eally likes playing
E ats nuts
L eaping about.

Brooke Millward (6)
Oakdene Primary School, Billingham

My Dog

M eat in the tin
Y ard it runs around in

D igs in the garden
O n my bed
G rowls at other dogs.

Rocco Khalili (6)
Oakdene Primary School, Billingham

Kieran

K is for keeping fit, I like playing tag
I is for ink, it is black
E is for eggs, they are nice
R is for red, I like it
A is for apple, it is my favourite fruit
N is for net, it is for catching things.

Kieran Ashe (7)
Princefield First School, Stafford

Strange Taste

Things in space
With a very strange taste.
A slimy ice cream
Will make you scream.
A metal stuffing
Makes you feel like a muffin
Triangle jelly makes you feel
Like there are aliens in your belly.
Things in space are made with a very strange taste.

Anna Young
St Joseph's Primary School, Newry

Stinger

S piky body
T elepathic ability
I nfra-red sun
N ice normally
G obbler
E vil face
R ude appearance.

Garyowen Nicolas
St Joseph's Primary School, Newry

When I Grow Up

When I grow up I wonder what kind of job I'll do?
Maybe I'll have one job then get another too.
I could be an astronaut and travel to the moon,
Or I could be a clown and inflate balloons!
I could be a train driver and transport cargo.
If I am an athlete I wonder where I'll go?
I could be an engineer and create cars,
Or I'll be a police officer and keep criminals behind bars.
When I grow up I wonder what kind of job I'll do?
Maybe I'll have one job then get another too.

Jack Mottram (9)
Scarcliffe Primary School, Chesterfield

Lost

I don't want to go to nursery
I have no power there
Only here with you
I lose my voice
I cannot find it anywhere
The bell rings
My name is called
Coat put on
My teacher gives out the letters and hands me back my voice
The door opens
I see Mummy
I hear my voice shout out
I'm here, I wave amongst the crowd
I've found myself again.

Shway Alexis
Talbot Primary School, Leeds

YOUNG WRITERS INFORMATION

We hope you have enjoyed reading this book – and that you will continue to in the coming years.

If you're a young writer who enjoys reading and creative writing, or the parent of an enthusiastic poet or story writer, do visit our website www.youngwriters.co.uk. Here you will find free competitions, workshops and games, as well as recommended reads, a poetry glossary and our blog.

If you would like to order further copies of this book, or any of our other titles, then please give us a call or visit **www.youngwriters.co.uk.**

Young Writers
Remus House
Coltsfoot Drive
Peterborough
PE2 9BF
(01733) 890066 / 898110
info@youngwriters.co.uk